# SPORTS HEROES AND LEGENDS

# Michael Jordan

**Read all of the books in this exciting, action-packed biography series!**

*Hank Aaron*

*Barry Bonds*

*Joe DiMaggio*

*Tim Duncan*

*Dale Earnhardt Jr.*

*Lou Gehrig*

*Mia Hamm*

*Tony Hawk*

*Derek Jeter*

*Michael Jordan*

*Michelle Kwan*

*Mickey Mantle*

*Shaquille O'Neal*

*Jesse Owens*

*Jackie Robinson*

*Babe Ruth*

*Ichiro Suzuki*

*Tiger Woods*

SPORTS HEROES AND LEGENDS

# Michael Jordan

## by Sean Adams

BARNES
&NOBLE

NEW YORK

*For Lee and Linda Adams, all-star parents (and in-laws!)*

**Cover photograph:**
**© David J. Phillip/AP Photos**

Barnes & Noble Publishing, Inc.
122 Fifth Avenue
New York, NY 10011

ISBN 0-7607-3467-4

Printed in the United States of America

05 06 07 08 MCH 11 10 9 8 7 6 5 4

Written by Liesa Abrams

Sports Heroes and Legends™ is a trademark of
Barnes & Noble Publishing, Inc.

# Contents

# "The Shot"

*Swish.*

The second the ball sank through the hoop, 19-year-old Michael Jordan's heart sank with it. It was March 29, 1982, and there were less than 60 seconds left in the NCAA championship game between Michael's team, the University of North Carolina Tar Heels, and their challengers, the Georgetown University Hoyas. Georgetown's center, Patrick Ewing, was already showing off the amazing toughness he would later be known for as a star player on the New York Knicks. Still, while Georgetown had controlled most of the game, the Tar Heels had pulled slightly ahead in the last few minutes.

But now Georgetown player Eric "Sleepy" Floyd's shot had just brought the score to 62–61. Michael's team was down by one point with no time to lose.

The Tar Heels' coach, Dean Smith, called a time-out, pausing the game to gather his team in a huddle and plan a comeback play. Michael knew that his coach was just as anxious about this next move as he and his teammates were. Smith had a big name in the world of college basketball and had already brought his teams to the Final Four five times and to the NCAA finals twice. But the one thing Smith didn't have was a championship win, and his eyes were on the prize.

Michael joined the huddle, figuring that any part he would have in Smith's play would involve getting the ball to one of his team's top scorers, James Worthy and Sam Perkins. It was what every player on the team expected to hear since the logical move in such a do-or-die moment would be to give the ball to a big playmaker.

But Dean Smith had a surprise in store for his team.

Yes, the expected move *would* be to let Worthy or Perkins take the shot, Smith agreed. But that was exactly why they shouldn't do it. Georgetown's coach, John Thompson, would expect it, too, and Thompson was sure to tell his strongest defensive players to swarm around James and Sam, as they'd been doing for most of the game. So the best hope the UNC Tar Heels had of clinching the championship game was to let their third-highest-scoring player take the shot instead.

Michael Jordan's heart began to race. As the lone freshman starter on a highly ranked college team, he was the third-leading scorer. Coach was putting the fate of this game in his hands.

"Make it, Michael," Coach Smith said as the team broke from their huddle.

Michael felt a chill run down his spine. Earlier, on the bus ride to the arena, he'd dreamed about sinking a game-winning shot. It was a common dream for a basketball player to have, he knew. It was every athlete's dream. But now he had the chance to make that dream a reality.

At the same time he also had the chance to lose, and lose big.

Michael gazed around the huge New Orleans Superdome. More than 61,000 fans were packed into the arena, and millions more were watching the game on TV. The next few seconds would decide whether Michael returned to his UNC campus as the hero who brought Dean Smith his first championship or the failure who cost his coach and his school a game that had been just within their reach.

The game clock started up, and Tar Heels guard Jimmy Black inbounded the ball to Michael at half-court. He and Jimmy passed the ball back and forth as they moved toward the basket, setting up the shot. When the Hoyas defense threatened Black, he tossed the ball to forward Matt Doherty. Doherty waited for Georgetown's players to set up under the basket to cover James Worthy and Sam Perkins, then returned the ball to Black. Black faked a pass toward the guys at the basket, then quickly threw the ball across the court to Michael Jordan—who was totally open.

But not for long!

As soon as the Georgetown players caught on, they rushed at Jordan, panicked. After witnessing Michael's performance in the game so far, they knew that he was every bit the threat to them right now that James Worthy could have been. Michael saw the defense coming at him but didn't flinch. The pressure was on, but he had been told to take the shot, and he would never disobey a coach's instructions.

Michael got a good look at the basket, then calmly took the jump shot from 16 feet away. The ball soared through the air, seeming to take hours to reach its destination.

*Swish.*

This time the sight of the ball sinking through the hoop filled Michael with an indescribable joy.

Georgetown got the ball back for the final seconds of the game but floundered their only attempt at a basket. The buzzer sounded, and Michael let out a triumphant, "It's over!" before rushing to hug Jimmy Black and Dean Smith.

The game may have been over, but Michael's fame and basketball glory were just beginning. "Your life will never be the same after that shot," Michael's father, James Jordan, told him. He had no idea how right he was.

# Chapter One

# Mini-Mike

It was love at first sight. The moment James Jordan, then a high school student, saw Deloris Peoples, he knew they were meant to be together. Within hours of meeting her, James confidently informed Deloris that he was going to marry her someday. Not only did his prediction come true, but the circumstances of their meeting proved that fate was at work in more than one way that day—James and Deloris met after attending a high school basketball game! What could be more perfect for the future parents of the greatest basketball player in history?

Several years later James and Deloris were married. After serving in the air force, James got a job with General Electric and the couple settled in North Carolina, where they had both grown up. The Jordans' family grew as children Ronald James, Deloris, and Larry were born. In 1963 Deloris was pregnant with their fourth child when James brought the family to Brooklyn,

The first official game of basketball was played in Springfield, Massachusetts, in the year 1892.

New York, so he could attend a General Electric training school that would help him advance in his job. That February 17, 1963, Deloris gave birth to Michael Jeffrey Jordan. But Michael didn't stay in New York for long. As soon as James had finished the training program, the Jordans returned to North Carolina, where Michael's younger sister, Roslyn, was later born.

James and Deloris were both the children of sharecroppers who paid their rent through sharing the produce they grew on their farms. James was determined that he would be the first in his family to own a home, and he and Deloris saved their money to buy a piece of land in Wilmington, North Carolina. James himself built the house he and his family would eventually live in, working hard at his job by day and spending evenings and weekends on construction, his children sometimes coming along to help. Meanwhile James continued to excel at General Electric as the years passed, receiving regular promotions, while Deloris also moved up in her job at the University of North Carolina Bank in Wilmington. Soon the family of seven was living quite comfortably.

Michael grew up admiring the way his parents always accomplished anything they set their minds to. "I learned the value of hard work and persistence from my family," Michael says. He also shares that it was James and Deloris who taught him, "You always have to focus in life on what you want to achieve."

Of course, the question sometimes is what, exactly, you want to achieve. And many might be surprised to know that for young Michael Jordan, being a basketball star was actually not his dream.

James Jordan was a huge sports fan, and sports and games were a big part of Michael's world as Michael grew up, from football in the backyard to checkers at the kitchen table. James's children had inherited his fierce competitive spirit, and they fought their hardest to win every time. As the youngest and smallest of the three boys, Michael had to fight extra hard and deal with losing repeatedly, giving him a toughness that would later become more important than he could ever imagine. Along with the family matches, Michael also played on school and local teams for lots of sports, but his favorite sport was . . .

Baseball.

That's right—when Michael Jordan started out, his dreams were not of one day playing in the NBA, but of growing up to be an All-Star pitcher for a major league baseball team.

7

In elementary school Michael joined his local Little League team, rotating positions between pitcher, shortstop, and out-field. He had a killer pitching arm and threw several no-hitters. Michael moved on from the Little League to the Babe Ruth League when he got older and soon became the star of his team. He was thrilled when they made it to the state champi-onship, but he never let the excitement break his concentration. His team won the championship, and Michael was given his first ever Most Valuable Player (MVP) award. That sealed the deal. Michael was convinced that he was well on his way to baseball stardom.

---

**66***My favorite childhood memory, my greatest achievement, was when I got the Most Valuable Player award when my Babe Ruth League team won the state championship. That was the first thing I accomplished in my life, and you always remember the first.***99**

—MICHAEL JORDAN

---

But baseball wasn't the only sport Michael enjoyed. Basketball was up there, too. His interest in the game got a jump start when his older brother Larry began playing, and James Jordan set up a basketball court in the family's backyard for the

Michael's first "hoop" was his trash can! When he was only five years old, he would get on his knees and dunk into the trash can in his bedroom.

brothers to play against each other. These matches could get pretty intense, and Michael, usually on the losing end, tried his best to learn his brother's skills and technique so he could be the winner someday. Of all the Jordans, Michael was probably the most competitive. He just couldn't stand losing. "I think Michael got so good because Larry used to beat him all the time," James later said, only half joking.

Larry was turning into a very talented basketball player, with an aggressive style and some unbelievable twists and turns on the court. Unfortunately, at five feet, eight inches tall, he just didn't have the reach to go the distance in the sport. Michael has often said that Larry would have been an NBA star, too, if he'd been taller. He's quick to admit that he learned his best moves from his older brother. "When you see me play, you see Larry play," Michael says.

In the early days, however, Michael was still shorter than Larry, and as much as he loved playing basketball and struggled to find a way to beat his brother, he couldn't see a future in the sport. Instead he continued to play as many sports as he could, working hard to be the best at each one.

Fred Lynch, Michael's basketball coach at D. C. Virgo Junior High, recalls that Michael was a good scorer for the team, playing point guard. At the same time Michael was quarterback for the football team and a pitcher and outfielder on the baseball team. Lynch was wowed by Michael's ability to handle some of the most important positions in three very different sports. In his opinion, it was possible for two reasons. "One was that Michael was very competitive," Lynch explains. "He hated losing, even then, and that made him work extremely hard when he played any of the sports." The other reason, Lynch believes, was the support Michael received from his parents, who had perfect attendance records for all of his games and always encouraged him to focus on the positive.

Then, during his sophomore year at Laney High School, Michael received some news that made it tough to look on the bright side—he didn't make the cut for the varsity basketball team. Michael had grown to five-foot eleven, three inches taller than Larry, whom he could now beat in their backyard games. But Michael's high school coach, Clifton Herring, thought Michael needed just a little more time on the JV team to rack up playing minutes and experience. Michael did his best to keep himself together around his friends, including best friend and teammate Leroy Smith. But later, in private, he broke down and cried, wondering if he should quit the game altogether. He just didn't believe in playing a sport he couldn't excel in.

Luckily the lessons Michael had learned from his parents came back to him. Would James or Deloris give up? No way. They would just get right back up and try harder. And that was exactly what Michael was going to do.

Michael pushed himself the whole year, averaging an impressive 28 points per game for the JV team. When he heard that the varsity team was calling up a JV player for the end of the season, which would include the state tournament, Michael was sure it would be him. So was Leroy Smith, who was as surprised as Michael to see his own name on the list instead. Even Leroy admitted that Michael could outplay him any day. But Leroy was six-foot five, towering a good six inches above Michael, and the team needed a big man.

Michael took the number 23 for his high school basketball jersey because it was roughly half of his older brother Larry's number, 45.

It was the second crushing blow of the basketball season for Michael, and he attended the state tournament as a substitute for a sick student manager, handing out towels to the players during the game. It was torture for Michael to watch the game from the bench, shut out from the action. "I made up my mind right then and there that this would never happen to me again," Michael has often said. "From that point on, I began working harder than ever on my basketball skills."

The work paid off, and so did all of the wishing Michael did to grow taller! James Jordan claims to have walked in on Michael actually hanging from a chin-up bar to stretch his body, and Michael laughingly admits it's true. Although he walked away from that bar with nothing but sore arms, Michael miraculously grew to six-foot three by his junior year! Now that he had the height to match his skills on the court, he easily made the varsity team. In fact, Michael not only made it, but was named starting point guard, a position that carries a ton of responsibility. The fall of his junior year, he made the tough decision to quit the football team so he could have more time to get in shape for basketball. As the season began, he was bursting to show everyone what he could do.

Unfortunately, he didn't get off to the best start on varsity. Michael wasn't aggressive enough in taking shots, and he made some mistakes. But he didn't let up on himself until he got better. Coach Herring and Fred Lynch, by then an assistant coach at Laney High, couldn't believe how hard Michael worked. Even though he wasn't on the JV team anymore, Michael showed up for their practice and did all of the drills and sprints, repeating the grueling workout with the varsity team during their practice directly afterward. "He'd also be in the gym Saturdays and Sundays, playing all day long," Lynch recalls.

Michael first picked up his famous trait of playing with his tongue hanging out of his mouth from his dad, who used to do the same thing while working on chores around the house. James says *he* inherited the habit from his own father.

Slowly Michael's confidence built, and his performance in the Laney High games showed it, like the way he could twist his body in mind-boggling directions to dodge defenders and make a shot. Most importantly, Michael developed an ability to stay calm under pressure. When the game was on the line, his focus and his play were even better than usual.

The game that Michael's high school coaches still talk about was part of a holiday tournament. Laney High was playing New Hanover in the final round, and the two Wilmington schools were huge rivals. During the first three quarters the game was a tug-of-war, with both teams evenly matched. By the fourth quarter Michael knew he had to do something—he had to make sure his team won this game. So he drove himself into action, stealing the ball from opposing players and making beautiful shot after beautiful shot. Amazingly, Michael scored the final 15 points for his team, including a game winner in the final second. Michael was ecstatic—he'd finally shown his family, teammates, and coaches that he was a true winner. He'd finally shown *himself* that he could live up to the potential he knew he had.

What Michael didn't know yet was that he'd shown this to some other people as well—including a few who would play a major role in his future.

# Chapter Two

# In the Zone

It all started with a phone call from the athletic director of the Wilmington County school system, Michael Brown, to Roy Williams, an assistant coach at the University of North Carolina. Brown had an urgent message for Williams—he had spotted a high school player who was unbelievable, out of this world. In fact, he told Williams, this Michael Jordan was possibly the best young athlete he'd ever seen. Williams jumped on the tip and quickly invited Michael to attend the basketball camp held by his boss, Dean Smith, at UNC. Every summer Smith's assistants would round up the best players they'd seen in North Carolina to come to the camp and show their stuff for the legendary coach, as well as learn the important fundamentals of the sport.

Michael couldn't have been more excited about the camp. The best part was that he wouldn't be going alone. Leroy Smith had been invited as well. The two friends arrived at the camp together, psyched for opening day, when they'd have the chance to play on the court where dozens of college stars had played before them. Michael was so pumped about being in the Tar Heels' Carmichael Gym that even though he was only asked to play two sessions—since the coaches had to give every camper some time on the court—he snuck back in for a third! Roy Williams noticed this but didn't object. He was impressed with Michael's ambition. And that wasn't all he was impressed with. After watching Michael play, Williams rushed over to another of Dean Smith's assistants and confided, "I think I've just looked at the best . . . high school player that I've ever seen."

Michael and Leroy roomed together at the camp, sharing a suite with two kids from Asheville, North Carolina—Randy Shepherd and Buzz Peterson. The four became joined at the hip, bonding over their shared love of basketball and dreams for the future. Still, there was something dividing them. "[Le]Roy and I were a notch or two down, and we understood this," Shepherd later said. "Michael and Buzz were just beginning to emerge. . . . They saw their destinies being very similar, and it pulled them towards each other."

Michael's destiny was taking off at amazing speed, and the next stop on the journey would be Howie Garfinkel's Five-Star Basketball Camp in Pittsburgh, Pennsylvania. The exclusive basketball camp had actually not invited Michael since—believe

In 1997 Coach Dean Smith became the winningest coach in Division I college basketball history after winning his 877th game.

it or not—he wasn't considered a top high school prospect! But Roy Williams knew better, and he wrangled a last minute invite to get Michael in.

Once Michael started playing, jaws started dropping. How could this kid be so good after playing just one year on varsity? Howie Garfinkel himself was blown away by Michael's abilities, saying it took watching only *one possession* to prove that Michael was a star in the making. During this particular play Michael was on defense, and he managed to steal the ball from the offensive player and streak back to the other end of the court. At the last second he had to put the brakes on his speed because dunking wasn't allowed at the camp. He slowed just in time to finish with a soft, easy, but precise basket.

Michael was as amazed at his accomplishments as everyone else. "I felt like someone had tapped me on the shoulder with a magic wand," he later said. He'd always been filled with the competitive drive to succeed and a confidence that he could do anything he set his mind to. But now, finally, he was discovering that he truly had the talent to match his spirit and dedication to the sport. By the end of Michael's stay at the Five-Star camp he'd been named Most Valuable Player and snagged 10 trophies for scoring, defense, and other accomplishments. The camp, Michael shares, "was the turning point in my life."

Back at Laney High for his senior year, the question now was where that turning point would send him. Michael led the Laney High Buccaneers to their first conference championship that year and finished second behind good friend Buzz Peterson in the voting for North Carolina High School Player of the Year. But his sights were already set beyond high school—Michael was ready for the NCAA. He'd always been a fan of North Carolina State, and he was also interested in the University of California at Los Angeles (UCLA). But Roy Williams had made up his mind. "We had decided that if we had been allowed only one player in the country, that player was going to be Michael Jordan," Williams later recalled. Williams and his boss, Dean Smith, did everything they could to convince Michael to accept a basketball scholarship from UNC. In the end, they got their wish, and Michael got his—he would be playing for a Division I school, the highest level of college ball.

Friends warned him that he'd be a benchwarmer as a freshman on a team already packed with more great players than they could use. Shouldn't he go somewhere else, where

Michael's speed was so amazing that during his freshman year at UNC, he was often mistakenly called for traveling because he appeared to be covering too much ground with the ball for the number of steps allowed. Once Coach Smith figured out the problem, he showed the referees the footage and put an end to the bad calls.

he'd have more playing minutes? "Everyone [in Wilmington] felt I was gonna go to North Carolina, sit on the bench for four years, then come back and work at a local gas station," Michael recalls. But he had faith in himself, and his goal wasn't to be the star on a midlevel team; it was all about winning, and he just wanted to be a part of a star *team*.

When Michael and his friend Buzz, who was also recruited by Smith, arrived in Chapel Hill, North Carolina, for their freshman year at UNC, neither expected the same glory they'd experienced as standout high school players. But Michael knew he had to be confident to gain his teammates' respect. Before practice officially began, he walked up to a group of players, including a couple of former Tar Heels who had graduated and were now in the NBA, and asked to join their pickup game. "I was so nervous, my hands were sweating," Michael later confessed. "I saw all these All-Americans, and I was just the lowest thing on the totem pole." But Michael blocked out his nerves and concentrated on the game. He paced himself, getting a feel for the other players, then finally broke loose and made one of the plays he was famous for—dodging and dunking over not one but *two* defenders, including the seven-foot-tall Geoff Compton.

Michael was still anxious for his first practice with the team, but the pickup game gave him the boost he needed to believe he really did belong with such talented players as James Worthy and Sam Perkins, who would both go on to the NBA. However, simply fitting in wasn't all Michael wanted—he was determined to win a starting position on the squad.

Michael knew he faced a real challenge. Dean Smith was tough on his players, making them pay their dues and earn every minute of playing time. Only three other freshmen had ever started a game for Coach Smith in the 21 years he'd been coaching at UNC. But as soon as Michael discovered that the one starting position open on the team was for second guard—the position he'd recently taken in high school—he had to go for it. So he pushed himself to be the best, proving to Smith in practice that he was undefeatable in any one-on-one match, including against players taller and bigger than he. Even an ankle injury that forced Michael to miss two weeks of practice didn't stop him from blowing Smith away. When the list of starting players went up right before the first game of the season, Michael's name was on it.

*Yes.* He'd done it!

Now his attention turned to the next goal—a winning season for the Tar Heels, starting with the opening game that night against Kansas. Michael began the game a little shaky, more nervous than he'd expected to be for his first college game, which took place in front of over 11,000 fans and was also broadcast on regional television. He missed his first shot, which he'd taken without his usual confidence. Immediately Michael knew he had to get back on track and focus, focus, focus. He went on to make his first basket of the game less than 60 seconds later. After that, he was in the zone. "As the game went on, I began to get more into the flow," Michael explained. "Once it was over, I realized I was just as good as anybody else." During his 31 minutes of playing time

Michael scored 12 points, helping the Tar Heels to their 74–67 victory over Kansas.

Michael's performance remained steady as the season continued, with his first standout game taking place before UNC fans at the home opener against the University of Tulsa. In his 22 minutes on the court Michael scored 22 points, made five rebounds and three assists, *and* stole the ball several times. His contribution to the Tar Heels' win of 78–70 was huge and proved that Michael did belong in the starting lineup.

Dean Smith was known for his Four Corners offensive strategy, which required all offensive players to score. During the 1981–82 season, Smith had the perfect team for this strategy—a group of talented players who could all perform on demand. No one star was going to have to break out and carry this team. The result was a strong season that led the Tar Heels to the 1982 NCAA championship. Michael, who had proudly accepted the honor of ACC—Atlantic Coast Conference—Rookie of the Year after the end of the regular season, went on to sink that dramatic winning basket in the championship game against Georgetown. The basket was soon nicknamed "The Shot" and earned Michael instant fame nationwide. Michael returned to the UNC campus for Michael Jordan Day and soon saw a picture of himself taking "The Shot" on the cover of the Chapel Hill phone book. "I think that shot really put

me on the map," Michael said. His friend Buzz went a step further, predicting that as big a basket as it was then, "in about ten
years, it will be even bigger."

While championships slipped just out of reach for Michael
and the Tar Heels his sophomore and junior years at UNC,
Michael continued to improve as a player—and the public
was taking notice. He was named College Player of the Year
by *Sporting News* magazine both years, praised for being a
well-rounded player who could not only score, but also dazzle
on defense and consistently come through when games were
on the line. During the summer after his sophomore year
Michael joined a team of college all-stars to travel to South
America and play in the Pan Am games. Along with being the
team's top scorer—leading the charge to the American gold
medal—Michael also realized he had a strong interest in the
world around him and decided to pick geography for his major
back at school.

Michael loved everything about UNC—the campus, the
classes, his friends, and most of all (of course) playing on

Michael remained so loyal to UNC that he wore his Tar Heels shorts underneath his Bulls uniform at every game.

Dean Smith's basketball team. But as his junior year was ending, Michael faced a tough decision. He had already proved himself in the world of college ball, and the NBA was showing serious interest in him. Should he leave college early and enter the NBA draft?

Michael struggled with the question, getting advice from his family, his friends, and especially his trusted coach, Dean Smith. As much as Smith hated to lose Michael, he always put his players' interests first. Another season at UNC meant possible injuries that could prevent Michael from ever playing in the NBA, and Smith assured Michael that he was 100 percent ready for the pros. Still, Michael ached to bring UNC one more championship before he left, and Deloris was wary of the idea of her son never finishing his degree. Michael was so torn that he kept Buzz up all night before the May 5 press conference where he was supposed to announce his decision and still hadn't made up his mind as he left the room that morning.

It was a last minute conversation with Dean Smith that finally helped Michael make a choice. Sitting in front of the reporters with Smith and his parents at his side, Michael finally let the world know that he was "coming out"—he was leaving UNC and making himself eligible to be drafted to an NBA team for the 1984–85 season.

Now it was Michael's turn to be in suspense—where would he end up playing in the fall?

# Chapter Three

# Rookie of the Year

The summer of 1984 was the most exciting of Michael's young life. The NBA draft was scheduled for June, and Michael was bursting to know which team he'd end up with— and also which pick he would be. As competitive as ever, Michael hoped to be chosen as early on as possible, definitely no lower than the fifth pick.

Meanwhile Michael had also been named cocaptain of the U.S. Olympic basketball squad, which would be competing in the Olympics that August in Los Angeles, and he was hard at work practicing. The squad was coached by Indiana Hoosiers coach Bobby Knight, whose team had taken down Michael's Tar Heels in the 1984 NCAA play-offs just months earlier. Knight was known for being a tough, even abusive coach who forced his players to stick to his system. However, when he looked at Michael, he saw a gold medal, so he relaxed his reins slightly and let Michael shine on the court. Surrounded by fellow college stars, including former Tar Heels teammate Sam Perkins and onetime challenger Patrick Ewing, Michael worked hard to ensure a win for his coach and his country. "Competing in the Olympics is a dream that I've had for a long time," he shared with pride.

With Michael, of course, the dream never stopped at competing—it was always about winning. Michael made sure his team did just that, helping them eliminate every competitor straight through to the gold medal match against Spain on August 10. Michael scored a team-high 20 points in the game, and the United States left the court with a 96–65 victory—and the gold medal.

---

*He's just the best player I've ever seen play.*

—BOBBY KNIGHT

---

"He's not human," Spain's coach, Antonio Diaz-Miguel, marveled. "He's a rubber man."

After the medal ceremony Michael searched the crowd for his mother and placed his medal around her neck. As always, he wanted to show the world what he never forgets—that each of his victories is shared with his parents.

In the first couple of months of Michael's rookie season with the Bulls, home attendance at Chicago Stadium nearly doubled, shooting from 6,365 a game to 12,763. By the end of the year it was up 87 percent. After three years sales of season tickets jumped from 2,047 (before Michael joined the team) to 11,000.

The gold medal turned out to be Michael's second triumph of the summer. Back in June, he'd gotten his wish—he'd gone as the third pick in the NBA draft. Why not first or second? Deep down, Michael couldn't help wondering the same thing, but the teams with the top two picks—the Houston Rockets and Portland Trailblazers—were both determined to add big players to their squads, so they went with six-foot-ten center Hakeem Olajuwon and seven-foot-one center and forward Sam Bowie, respectively. So Michael was headed to Chicago to play with the Chicago Bulls. Michael had never even been to Chicago, and he knew he was joining a troubled team. In the previous 10 years the Bulls had only three winning seasons. But Michael loved a good challenge; he was ready to turn the Bulls around.

Michael would soon find out just how hard a job he'd taken on. In the first official game of the season, against the Washington Bullets, Michael was given a rough reminder that he had to adjust to a different type of game now that he had joined the pros. "During the first few minutes, I was knocked to the floor," Michael remembers. "It was then that I learned that basketball is a game of strength." Michael was still pretty thin, and he realized he'd have to bulk up if he wanted to withstand the beatings NBA players regularly face on the court.

As the season wore on, Michael continued to file away the lessons he picked up from his experience as a professional player while dazzling spectators with his powerful slam dunks, unbelievable speed, and stunning moves on the court. As hard as he tried to be just one member of a team and fulfill the promise he'd made before the start of the season that "[the Bulls] won't be the Michael Jordan show," reporters still nicknamed the team "Michael and the Jordanaires," and Michael was undeniably the star of the team and the reason for their new success.

Michael's unbelievable performance didn't go unnoticed, and even though he was just a rookie, he was voted onto that year's All-Star team. Unfortunately, many of the veteran players in the game seemed to resent Michael's quick rise to fame—and fortune. Before the season had even begun, Michael had been given an endorsement deal with Nike worth more money than any other deal like it, including the deals his fellow All-Star players had. Here was this new kid getting all kinds of money and attention thrown at him when the older players

Michael's initial contract with the Bulls included a special "love of the game clause" that allowed him to play pickup basketball games, something usually off-limits to NBA players because of the risk of injury. Michael insisted on the clause because he could never give up the freedom to play the game he loved whenever and wherever he wanted.

had been working hard for years. They assumed he must be seriously cocky and supposedly agreed before the All-Star game to freeze Michael out of the action, rarely passing him the ball and coming down extra hard on defense. Michael was crushed. He'd been so excited about his first chance to play in an All-Star game with players he admired so much. "That incident was one of the most painful experiences of my life to that point," Michael later wrote. "I was so disillusioned I didn't know what to do."

But disappointment quickly turned to inspiration, as it always did for Michael. After he heard that Detroit Pistons player Isaiah Thomas was reportedly behind the "freeze out," Michael made sure to lead the Bulls to a decisive victory against the Pistons in their next regular season game, contributing a whopping 49 points and 15 rebounds.

Nike's Air Jordan sneakers, released during Michael's rookie year, were an immediate success, grossing $130 million in record time. They went on to become the best-selling sneakers in history.

While Michael's efforts throughout the season brought the Bulls to the play-offs for the first time in several years, the team was eliminated in the first round against the Milwaukee Bucks. Still, Michael's first NBA season had been a success. He finished the year with an impressive scoring average of 28.2 points per game and solid numbers in assists and rebounds, even though he was one of the shorter players on the court. He was named NBA Rookie of the Year, an honor that meant a lot to him but wasn't the award he truly longed for.

Michael wanted a championship ring, and he was determined to turn the Bulls into a team that could help him get one.

As the following season began, Michael realized that seeing that dream come true in 1986 was a long shot. The Bulls lost their first eight exhibition games (warm-up games that don't count as part of the regular season). Michael was frustrated but continued to push himself and his teammates to shape up. They managed to win their first two official games of the season.

However, during the second period of their third game, against the Golden State Warriors, Michael took a fall. When he finally got up, he was limping. Michael's worst fears were soon confirmed when he learned he had a small break in his left foot. He would be out for a large chunk of the season.

Michael was heartbroken. Basketball was everything to him, and he'd never felt as helpless as he did then, sitting on the bench and watching his teammates play without him. "I've never gone through anything like this before," he said at the time. "And I don't really know how to deal with it." Finally Michael received permission to return to North Carolina until his foot had healed, where he was able to earn the credits he still needed for his college diploma. At least he could keep the promise he'd made to his mother when he left UNC to someday get his degree, but as the months went by, his longing to be out on the basketball court—his home—became unbearable. Every time Michael went in for a checkup, he would hold his breath nervously, only to be told again and again that he wasn't healing as quickly as the doctors had hoped. The experience was pure agony for him. "My body could stand the crutches, but my mind couldn't stand the sidelines," he explained.

In all, Michael missed 64 games—of which the Bulls won only 21. It wasn't until March 15, 1986, that Michael finally rejoined his teammates on the floor of Chicago Stadium. Even then the team management limited his playing time to just seven minutes a half, claiming Michael still needed to go easy on his foot. But Michael made those minutes count, and once he was allowed back in the starting lineup in April, he helped the Bulls just barely make it into the play-offs.

Since the Bulls had the worst record of the Eastern Division teams in the play-offs, they would face the top team, the Boston Celtics, in the first round. Even with Michael Jordan back in action, no one expected the Bulls could defeat the Celtics, led by superstar Larry Bird. But Michael always went into every game believing he could win, and he certainly did what he could to make it happen, contributing 49 points in game one. Still, the Celtics were the stronger team, and they took the game 134–104.

Time for game two—and Michael's determination had only grown stronger. He was pure magic on the court, dodging every Celtic player assigned to guard him, including one of the best defensive players in the league, Dennis Johnson. Michael alone sent the game into double overtime, scoring a play-off record-making 63 points. No one could believe what they were watching was real!

Sadly, Michael's incredible performance wasn't enough to rescue the game, and the Celtics still pulled off a 135–131 victory. Some people figured Michael would be okay with the loss since it was still his mind-blowing moves that everyone was talking about, not the fact that the Celtics had won the game. Even the Celtics couldn't stop shaking their heads in awe. Boston's coach told reporters that unlike usual—when his players on the bench would strain to make eye contact with him, hoping to be put into the game—every time he glanced down the line, the players would lean back, dreading having to try to guard Michael. Defensive star Dennis Johnson admitted, "I wasn't guarding him. No one was guarding him. No one *can* guard him."

But Michael wasn't interested in the compliments, the amazement, or the personal glory. All he'd wanted was to help

---

**❝**I don't want anyone to feel that I have a weakness. . . . If you push me toward something that you think is a weakness, then I will turn that weakness into a strength.**❞**

—MICHAEL JORDAN

---

his team win, and it hadn't happened. "I'd give all the points back if we could win," he said.

As expected, the Bulls were eliminated in the next play-off game. It had been a long and rough season for Michael, full of disappointment and heartache. But he did know that everything he'd been through had only made him stronger, and one of these years he was going to make it to the championship game—and win.

# Chapter Four

# Slam Dunk

**M**ichael entered the 1986–87 season feeling energized. His foot was fully healed, and he knew nothing could hold him back. Individually, nothing did—Michael won the NBA scoring title for the first time, racking up more points during the season than any other player in the league. Michael was especially proud of his accomplishments on defense because they proved he was about more than just scoring. That season he set a new record for having over 200 steals *and* over 100 blocked shots in one season. His 125 blocked shots actually topped the number of blocks made by 13 of the NBA's giant centers! However, Michael's efforts weren't enough to help the Bulls make it any further than they had the previous year. Once again they were eliminated in the first round of the play-offs by the Celtics.

Michael continued to sharpen every aspect of his game the following season, and the awards just wouldn't stop coming. He

The incredible jumps and leaps that made Michael famous have been measured, showing that Michael is able to leap an amazing 44 inches off the ground. Studying Michael's "hang time" across his first five NBA seasons, air force physics professor Lieutenant Colonel Douglas Kirkpatrick calculated that Michael spent more than 90 minutes of those years in the air!

repeated as the leading scorer of his team and the league and again broke through the 200-steals-and-100-blocked-shots ceiling. However, this season he added some new honors to the list—NBA Most Valuable Player as well as MVP of the All-Star game and Defensive Player of the Year. "The one award that meant the most to me during my career was being named Defensive Player of the Year," Michael later shared, after numerous other awards had been heaped upon him. "Before that year no one ever had been named Most Valuable Player and Defensive Player of the Year [in the same season], much less lead the league in scoring and steals. That award made a statement about what I was about."

Michael dared anyone to say he wasn't a well-rounded player now!

No one argued with the fact that Michael was a basketball god, but what some people *did* question was whether that was enough to give him and his team what they longed for—a championship win. The 1987–88 season ended in disappointment yet again. The Bulls advanced to the second round of the play-offs for the first time in Michael's years with the team, but they lost in that round to the Detroit Pistons.

---

*If you can defense Michael Jordan, you can defense anyone in the league—anyone in the* world!

—DENNIS RODMAN

---

There's a well-known saying in the basketball world that the team with the league's leading scorer can never win a championship because a winning team needs to be made up of a group of talented players who can work well together, not just one star. It drove Michael crazy to hear people say that about him and the Bulls—especially when his personal hero, Julius Erving (Dr. J to sports fans), even said that until the Bulls won a championship, Michael couldn't be seen at the same level as champion players Magic Johnson and Larry Bird. Michael tried to point out there was a big difference between his "supporting cast" and the talented Laker and Celtic players Johnson and Bird had been surrounded by. In response the Bulls management worked to build a solid team around Michael, and Michael was

When *World Book Encyclopedia* released its 1988 edition, Michael Jordan was among the 70 new entries included.

psyched when he realized that the team's 1987 draft picks, forwards Scottie Pippen and Horace Grant, could be exactly what the Bulls needed. Seven-foot-one-inch center Bill Cartwright was also added to the Bulls lineup in 1988, giving the team some extra height.

In the spring of 1989 Michael Jordan's Bulls made it to their first Eastern Conference finals, where they faced their previous year's rivals, the Detroit Pistons, for the Eastern Conference title and the chance to go to the NBA championship. The Pistons were an extraordinarily physical team, nicknamed the "Bad Boys" of the league for their rough style on the court. They developed a defensive strategy against Michael called "the Jordan Rules," which basically involved doing anything possible with their size and toughness to shut Michael down. Through aggressively keeping Michael away from the basket, the Pistons managed to defeat the Bulls four games to two, then went on to sweep the NBA championship series against the Los Angeles Lakers.

Michael was incredibly frustrated at the loss, especially because he had finally come so close to his dream. But he knew that he and his team were getting stronger all the time, and only a few more changes would allow them to reach their goal.

One very important change came before the start of the 1989–90 season, when Phil Jackson was named head coach of the Bulls, replacing Doug Collins. Jackson, once a player on a championship New York Knicks team, was determined to find a way to make the Bulls work well as a team and not just rely on Michael's abilities. He began using assistant coach Tex Winter's "triangle offense" system, nicknamed "the triangle." Jackson wanted to create a situation on the court where if (or actually, more like *when!*) Michael was double- or even triple-teamed, there were other offensive players prepared to make the baskets.

---

**❝**He's the only player in the game who has no weaknesses.**❞**

—Danny Ainge, then guard for the Portland Trailblazers, after Michael was named MVP for the 1990–91 season.

---

"In the beginning, I fought the triangle," Michael admits. "I thought Phil believed all the talk about not being able to win

In 1988 Michael Jordan became the first basketball player ever to appear on a Wheaties cereal box.

a championship with me leading the league in scoring. I thought he went to that offense to take the ball out of my hands." Michael wasn't a selfish ballplayer, as some people thought—his goal was always to do what was best for the team. "I'd rather score 10 points less a game and win 20 more games a year," Michael insists. It was just that in the past, taking the shots himself had been the Bulls' best bet at winning, and he worried that the triangle would hurt their chances. Still, Michael had always shown his coaches complete respect, and he and his teammates worked hard to learn how to win as a team with the new system.

By the end of the season the Bulls were coming together, ready to overcome their reputation as a one-man team. Matched up against the Pistons again in a battle for the Eastern Conference title, Michael and the rest of his team fought hard not to let "the Jordan Rules" defeat them. Playing against a confident team of defending champions, the Bulls kept the series a tug-of-war, making the Pistons play all seven games. But in the crucial game seven the Bulls fell to the Pistons, and Detroit enjoyed their second NBA championship, this time winning it from the Portland Trailblazers.

For many athletes six years of last minute disappointment and frustrating near misses would be too much. For Michael Jordan, especially, it became harder and harder to be put on this pedestal above all other basketball players but at the same time be written off as someone who wasn't valuable to a team—the single most important thing to him. But Michael never lost his love of the game or his passion to play his hardest every moment. Most importantly, Michael never lost faith that one day he would prove the doubters wrong.

---

❝I don't always have to hit the last shot, but I do have to walk away knowing I did everything I could to win the game.❞

—MICHAEL JORDAN

---

As the 1990–91 season progressed, Michael had every reason to believe in himself. His life off the court was going great. In 1989 Michael had married his girlfriend of several years, Juanita Vanoy, sharing how much it meant to him that "she really cared about me as a person, not because I played for the Bulls." Their first child, Jeffrey Michael Jordan, was now a small

Between 1987 and 1989 the Bulls had more sellout games than in the previous 22 years.

toddler, and Michael—ever a family man—got a huge kick out of being able to pass on everything his own father had given him during his childhood. "I'm so proud of being a father," Michael boasted. "The feeling is indescribable."

Meanwhile Michael was once again racking up the on-court accomplishments—only this year he was receiving plenty of support from his teammates. When the regular season ended, Michael led the league in scoring for the fifth time in a row, but Scottie Pippen and Horace Grant also had impressive points-per-game averages. "Things have changed," Michael told reporters. "A few guys have emerged, a few guys have matured, and we're a team now." Michael was so thrilled at the way the Bulls were coming together that when he was given his second MVP award, he asked his teammates to come on the court with him. Accepting the trophy, Michael humbly announced that "most of the credit . . . should go to my teammates, who have stepped up and put us in this position."

The Bulls swept their first play-off series, against the New York Knicks, then moved on to play the Philadelphia 76ers in the second round, defeating them four games to one. The Bulls had made it to the Eastern Conference finals for the third consecutive year—and were once again matched up against the Detroit Piston "Bad Boys."

But this time the Bulls were ready. Playing a balanced game where the contributions of several other players were as important as Michael's, the Bulls' quick offense and solid defense led them to a full-on sweep—they eliminated the Pistons four games to none. A triumphant Michael rejoiced in finally having trounced the Pistons, repeatedly crediting his teammates with having made the victory possible. "I've always wanted to simply be part of a team," Michael insisted, and for the first time it looked like he'd gotten his wish.

Michael's true dream, of course, was still to win the championship—and now he and the Bulls would get the chance. But their opponents in the championship series were the talented and experienced Los Angeles Lakers, led by Michael's hero Magic Johnson. Did Michael and the rest of the Bulls have what it takes to beat a team of champions? They were about to find out.

# Chapter Five

# Dream Teams

The Los Angeles Lakers had been called the "Team of the 80s" because they'd dominated the league during the decade, winning three championships. Superstar guard Magic Johnson was supported by Michael's talented Tar Heels teammates Sam Perkins and James Worthy and a strong bench that could be counted on when the Lakers needed help.

But Michael was pumped for the challenge. He knew that a championship win against such a powerhouse team, led by a star like Magic, would finally give him and his Bulls the recognition and respect he longed for. Besides, it was 1991—time for a new team to take center stage. "I've been waiting six years to get to this point," Michael said. "We're here. We can't let it get away from us."

At first, however, it looked like that might just happen. Game one ended in a disappointing loss for the Bulls. Michael counted on himself to make clutch baskets, and his heart fell when the 18-foot jumper he took in the last seconds of the game bounced back out of the rim after seeming like a sure thing. "We had every opportunity to win," Michael said after the game. "But I missed my last two shots."

If the Lakers were encouraged by their victory, then they obviously didn't get how Michael works. The Bulls came back to crush the Lakers in game two, with a final score of 107–86. Michael's 33 points were a major factor in the win, but so were the double figures of Scottie Pippen, Horace Grant, and John Paxson. Game three was closer, but after the hotly contested game went into overtime, the Bulls snagged a 104–96 win. Game four also went to the Bulls, and Michael was bursting with excitement as he walked onto the court for the fifth game of the finals. A championship was finally within his reach—just one win away!

The pressure was on, and this time the Lakers stayed neck and neck with the Bulls for much of the game. But Michael no longer felt he had to carry his team. The Bulls had learned how to play together and trust one another in key moments, which would now prove crucial. With under a minute left to play in the fourth quarter of game five, the Bulls had only a two-point lead over the Lakers. Michael had the ball in his hands, and he drove toward the basket but was instantly surrounded by Laker defenders. Quickly Michael made a blind pass directly behind him to where he knew his teammate John Paxson was waiting. Paxson caught the ball and took the shot, giving the Bulls enough of a lead to clinch the game.

The Bulls had done it! They were NBA champions!

Michael collapsed in tears of joy back in the locker room after being presented with the trophy by NBA commissioner David Stern. "This is the most proud day I've ever had," he said, the emotions still overwhelming him. The victory was especially sweet, he stated, because the Bulls had made this happen as a team. "It was a seven-year struggle," he continued. "Now we can get rid of the stigma of the one-man team. We did it as a team all season long. I played my game, but with their efforts, we were a better team."

With an NBA title under their belt, the Bulls entered the 1991–92 season confident and raring to go. "Now that he's gotten over the burden of winning a championship," James Jordan warned, "Michael can play a lot more relaxed. Totally relaxed, and that's a scary situation."

It didn't take long for Michael to prove his dad right. Led by Michael's spectacular play, the Bulls took the top spot in the Central Division after their seventh game of the season and held on for the rest of the year, despite constant challenges. "Every team is playing us really tough because we're the defending champs," Michael explained. "We're the guys to beat."

When the Bulls came back from a 15-point deficit to beat the Trailblazers in the fourth quarter of game six of the 1992 finals, they were the first team in history to overcome a gap that wide in the last quarter of a final game.

They may have been the team to beat, but they weren't beaten very often, even earning the nickname "the Unbeata-Bulls" from one sportswriter. The team finished the season with 67 wins and only 15 losses, the best record in Bulls history. Michael had his sixth-straight scoring title, but his points-per-game average was one of the lowest of his career until then at 30.1, proving that he had involved his teammates in games more than ever.

The 1992 play-offs showcased both Michael's talent and toughness and the skill and abilities of the entire Bulls team. The Bulls swept the Miami Heat in the first round, and Michael topped his own previous record for three-game scoring with a massive total of 135 points. The Eastern Conference semifinals against the New York Knicks didn't go quite as smoothly, as the Knicks stretched the series all the way to a seventh game. But Michael received solid support from his teammates, and the Bulls managed to win the deciding game seven. "New York deserves credit," Michael acknowledged, always quick to praise other players. "They woke us up."

If the Bulls weren't wide awake and hungry for a second championship before the series against the Knicks, they were now. The Bulls beat their next challengers, the Cleveland Cavaliers, in six games. Next they moved on to the NBA finals for the second year in a row, this time going up against the Portland Trailblazers—a team that had once had the chance to draft Michael and passed, giving him extra motivation to put them in their place. On top of that, the Trailblazers' star guard, Clyde Drexler, had finished second to Michael in the voting for that year's regular season MVP. No way would Michael give anyone the chance to say his runner-up had deserved the award more. "With all the hype about Clyde and myself, that's the competition I need to raise my game," Michael said.

The Blazers didn't make it easy for their opponents—Portland started out matching each Bulls victory with a win of their own, taking the second and fourth games. The Bulls won game five, leaving them one game shy of a second championship, but Michael knew they couldn't afford overconfidence. "We know how close we are, but the closer you are, the harder it is."

Michael was so determined to show his appreciation for the hard work and quality play of his teammates after the 1990–91 season that when he won MVP of the finals, he refused to do the traditional Walt Disney World commercial alone and instead insisted that the entire starting lineup of the Bulls be featured in the ad and split the $100,000 paycheck equally.

Still, as the Bulls returned to Chicago Stadium for the sixth game of the series, they couldn't help imagining the excitement of winning the finals on home turf this time, since last year's clincher had taken place in Los Angeles. They wouldn't have to imagine for long—the Bulls won the game 97–93, joining an elite list of teams (the Celtics, Lakers, and Pistons) that had accomplished back-to-back championships. Once again

Michael shared the glory with his teammates, especially the reserves who'd played very well in the all-important sixth game. "Everybody contributed," he commented. "These guys really carried us. It was a good team effort."

Michael couldn't have been happier with his Bulls team, but he was also very excited to play with a different team during the upcoming summer—the U.S. Olympic team, which for the first time ever was allowing professional players to compete. "When I got the opportunity to play in the Olympics when I was in college, it was a dream come true," Michael said. "Now I get to do it twice. It's very rare that people get to do something of this stature twice."

Michael was happy to be joined on the squad by Bulls teammate Scottie Pippen but especially psyched about the chance to play alongside the other basketball greats who had so far only faced him down on the court. "It's . . . an opportunity to get to know many great athletes I normally compete against all year long and meet them in a social atmosphere." The team

The 1992 Olympic Dream Team's 127 points against Brazil set the record for the most points ever scored in an Olympic basketball game.

that would later be called "the Dream Team" included veteran superstars Magic Johnson and Larry Bird as well as more recent and emerging dynamos Patrick Ewing, Charles Barkley, Clyde Drexler, Karl Malone, John Stockton, David Robinson, Chris Mullin, and one college player—Duke University star Christian Laettner. "This team has a mystique of quality built up over 15 years," said Coach Chuck Daly. "It won't be like this again."

---

**❝**I think that's what makes the Dream Team so special—because it's a once-in-a-lifetime situation.**❞**

—Michael Jordan

---

Daly was right about his one-of-a-kind squad. The Dream Team earned its nickname, winning all eight of its games. Michael relaxed, letting his supremely talented teammates do much of the scoring. But he was unable to resist pushing a little harder in the gold medal game against the Croatian team, pouring in the most points of his team—22—to help the United States to a 117–85 victory. Michael was thrilled to have won his second Olympic gold medal but also enjoyed the experience on a more personal level. "The relationship with the players has been really more than I expected," he commented. "It's been great."

As exciting as Michael's back-to-back championships and Olympic gold medals were, some wondered if it would be too much for the athlete. Michael and Scottie were both starting the 1992–93 season without the benefit of a restful summer off, and the pressure was on them to reach an accomplishment that hadn't been achieved by any team in recent history— a *three-peat*.

# Chapter Six

# Out of Left Field

**M**ichael's pure love of basketball was matched only by his desire to win, to smash records and continually achieve the impossible—or at least the improbable. He had just one thing on his mind as the 1992–93 season began: Michael was determined to set himself apart from the basketball heroes of his time, Magic Johnson and Larry Bird, and help his team win a third-straight NBA championship title.

The season provided more challenges than Michael had anticipated. "I knew it was going to be tough this year," he admitted, "but frankly, it's been tougher than I thought. We're physically and mentally fatigued, and we're a little out of sync from time to time." In fact, the season turned out to be the first in several years that Michael wasn't named Most Valuable Player at the end of the regular season. The award went to Charles Barkley of the Phoenix Suns.

Michael's 41-point-per-game average during the 1993 finals against the Phoenix Suns set an NBA finals record.

But when play-off time rolled around, the Bulls rallied themselves to act like the champions they were, taking down Atlanta, Cleveland, and New York as easy as one, two, three. For the third year in a row the Bulls were going to the NBA finals! But many doubted that the Bulls could pull off another championship, especially considering who their opponents were—the Phoenix Suns. Not only did Phoenix have the year's MVP, but the team also had the best record in the league that season. Barkley was joined by All-Star Dan Majerle and a solid supporting cast of players.

But Michael prided himself on coming through when his team needed him most, and this series was one of those times. "It's all about making history now," Michael said at the first game of the finals. "We're here to make history."

Michael's teammates listened, and the Bulls took games one and two, gearing up to seal the deal in games three and four back home in Chicago. But Phoenix wasn't ready to give up that easily, and they pushed game three into *triple* overtime,

Twelve-year-old Michael at bat for his Babe Ruth baseball team.

High school standout Michael Jordan on his signing day for Dean Smith and the UNC-Chapel Hill Tar Heels basketball squad.

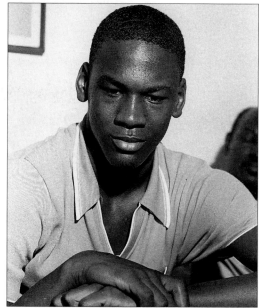

Taking it to the hoop for the Tar Heels.

Michael and UNC coach Dean Smith at the May 5, 1984 press conference at which Michael announced he would enter the NBA draft.

This Canadian player's defense is no match for Michael, who easily overtakes him to shoot in this 1984 Summer Olympic Game.

Michael and his family attend a victory rally in Chicago on June 14, 1991, after he helped the Bulls win the NBA title.

Dunking the ball during Game 6 of the 1993 NBA Finals

Michael at batting practice on his first day of training camp with the Chicago White Sox, February 18, 1995.

Soaring high above the rest in this 1997 Bulls-Utah Jazz game

Michael scores his thirty thousandth career point in this January 2002 game against his old team, the Chicago Bulls— joining Kareem Abdul-Jabbar, Wilt Chamberlain, and Karl Malone as the only players in history to reach that mark.

walking away with a 129–121 victory. Michael realized his dream was on the line, and he fought back with a vengeance in game four, knocking down basket after basket for a total of 55 points to help his team hold on to the edge in the series. Every nerve in Michael's body was charged as he went into game five, knowing the Bulls were just one win away from a three-peat. But the Suns got in another victory, sending the series back to Phoenix for game six.

This was it, Michael knew. If he wanted to defend his NBA title, it was now or never—even with the extra challenge of winning on enemy turf. The Bulls played hard, but the Suns came right back, answering Chicago's baskets with their own. It came down to the final minutes, and the Bulls were down by four. So what did Michael do? Score, of course! Michael's layup closed the gap to two points, and then John Paxson went on to hit a three pointer at the buzzer, giving the Bulls a 99–98 victory.

Michael and the Bulls had their three-peat!

"Winning this championship is harder than anything I've ever done in basketball," Michael said. But in his mind the tougher the fight, the sweeter the victory. Looking at his life at that moment, Michael couldn't imagine it any fuller. His list of achievements on the court over the last nine years seemed nearly endless. He was already being called the best basketball player ever. Meanwhile Michael and Juanita's family had grown to include son Marcus James and daughter Jasmine. As Michael thought about what was next for him, he wondered if he needed a new challenge.

Then in July 1993 Michael faced a different and unexpected challenge—one that would turn his world upside down and leave him a changed man forever. James Jordan, Michael's father and the man he called his best friend, was murdered by muggers in North Carolina. The entire Jordan family was devastated, and Michael in particular reeled from the loss, having to adjust to living without the man he'd always looked to for advice and guidance, the man who "knew everything about me." Later Michael reflected on how his father's death affected his life going forward. "I had to make the kind of decisions men make, and I had to make them for myself without that shoulder to lean on."

The first major decision Michael made was one that stunned and disappointed many sports fans. In October of 1993 Michael announced that he was retiring from basketball. "I love the game and I always will," he said. But Michael had a new understanding of just how precious the time he had with his family was and how easily it could all end without warning. "There are times in one's life when you have to put games aside," he explained.

Despite this statement, many wondered just how long an athlete as driven and passionate as Michael Jordan could stay in retirement. Soon Michael did grow restless to compete in a sport he loved, and he decided to get back in the game. But the game he returned to shocked the entire nation. Michael was playing *baseball*.

"My father and I talked about baseball all the time," Michael later admitted, explaining that it had been a dream of James Jordan's to see his son join the ranks of athletes like Bo Jackson who were able to play in more than one professional sport. As a child, Michael had juggled baseball and basketball and played well in both games. But he hadn't played baseball since high school. Now his body was conditioned for basketball, a sport that calls for a different build and a different type of strength. Michael was also 31 years old, a bit late to begin training for an entirely new and extremely difficult sport. Still, Michael had a tried-and-true way of dealing with doubters—he just let their comments motivate him to push harder. "I always considered myself a great all-around

❝*[Michael] brings something to the clubhouse that we haven't had. When you're around a true winner, you can tell it. We love it. [Having a superstar here] hasn't been a distraction at all.*❞
—WHITE SOX PLAYER FRANK THOMAS

athlete," he explained, "and I believed I could do anything if I set my mind to it."

"Michael likes challenges," Bulls owner Jerry Reinsdorf chimed in. "He likes to do what people say he can't do." Reinsdorf continued to support his basketball star even after Michael left the Bulls, giving him the opportunity to practice with the *other* Chicago sports club he owned—the White Sox major league baseball team. When Michael arrived for the team's spring training in Florida he was bursting with excitement. This was a chance to go back to his roots, to remember what it was like to have to fight for success in a brand-new and unfamiliar world.

But the fight turned out to be tougher than Michael expected. He managed to hold his own in spring training, but it quickly became clear that he wasn't ready for the major leagues and would have to play on a minor league team, ending up with the Birmingham Barons in Alabama, a Double-A team associated with the White Sox.

---

**"**If anyone didn't think I was serious [about baseball], it was because they could not see the blood dripping off my hands, or those six A.M. batting sessions.**"**

—Michael Jordan

---

Television ratings for NBA basketball dropped 31 percent in the first year Michael was retired from the Bulls.

Michael's first official game with the Barons took place on April 8, 1994, and even though he had a few chances at bat, he went hitless. Michael was disappointed in his performance, but it didn't put a dent in his resolve to keep working hard at baseball. "They told me there would be nights like this," he said. "But what I learned in basketball is that you have to have resiliency."

Resiliency had never been a problem for Michael, and he kept pushing himself, making sure he was the first to arrive and the last to leave for every team practice. He struggled to block out the added pressure of the extraordinary amount of attention focused on his baseball career, wishing he could be just another minor league player hoping to make it to "the Show," as the major leagues are often called.

As the baseball season stretched on, this dream started to seem out of reach for Michael. He had several shining moments on the field and gave everything he could. But by the end of the season his statistics were low, something Michael definitely wasn't used to. Still, he wasn't ready to give up that easily. "I can

Chicago Stadium may have been torn down, but the gym's wooden floor with the Bulls logo is now in Michael's home—it serves as the floor in his trophy room, which holds quite a few trophies!

accept failure, but I can't accept not trying," he explained. So he joined another minor league team in the Arizona Fall League, the Scottsdale Scorpions, to continue working on his game that fall.

Meanwhile basketball fans who'd been suffering from Michael withdrawal went crazy when it was announced at the last minute that Michael would join other NBA players in a charity game sponsored by his Bulls teammate Scottie Pippen at the soon-to-be-demolished Chicago Stadium on September 9, 1994. The Bulls had been knocked out of the '94 conference finals the previous spring by the Knicks, but Scottie had continued to be a strong player even without Michael at his side. Michael was proud of him and happy to help out for a good cause.

Michael was also thrilled, deep down, to be on a professional basketball court again—and it showed. During the game he let loose, putting on a great show. While the game was for fun and little effort was made on defense, Michael's 52 points still made him the top scorer that night. After the game Michael became emotional over the knowledge that this stadium, where he'd lived so many of his dreams—where his father had *watched* him live those dreams—would be torn down. Before leaving the court, he bent down to kiss the floor.

The night was a splashy reminder to Michael of what he'd walked away from and a heartbreaking reminder to fans of what they were missing. But Michael hoped that the fans would understand the importance he placed on not giving up. It wasn't in Michael to walk away from something until he felt he'd truly given it his all. At the same time baseball was offering Michael a way to come to peace with the loss of his father, to work through his grief by living out an idea he and James had shared in private for years. "What baseball did for me was give me an opportunity to revisit all those moments that I had with my father," Michael later admitted. In a way, Michael's time on the baseball field allowed him to really say good-bye.

---

❝*If I wouldn't have [played baseball after retiring from basketball], there's no way I would have been able to come back to the game of basketball.*❞

—MICHAEL JORDAN

---

But inside him, something was slowly being reborn—his pure love of the game of basketball and a longing to be back on the court, fighting for a win. When the major league baseball players went on strike, leaving the baseball world in an upheaval, Michael officially retired from the minor league. Almost immediately the buzz began—if Michael was leaving baseball, did that mean he'd return to basketball?

At first the question remained unanswered. Then Michael started dropping hints. He called his former Bulls teammate B. J. Armstrong at seven A.M. one morning and asked to meet for breakfast. The breakfast invitation quickly turned into a suggestion that they go to the gym and mess around with the ball. "Messing around" became a one-on-one competition on the court, and Armstrong sensed that Michael was testing himself, seeing if he still had it in him. Soon afterward Michael began actually attending Bulls practices, doing the drills along with the team.

Just when Michael's fans could barely contain their excitement and curiosity, Michael at last satisfied the hungry public with two simple, thrilling words:

"I'm back."

# Chapter Seven

# Rebound

On March 19, 1995, Michael played in his first NBA game since the 1993 championships. The Bulls were facing the Indiana Pacers on the Pacers' turf, but fans still cheered wildly for the return of their opposing team's hero. Michael was no longer number 23—instead he wore the number he'd worn in baseball, number 45. He looked at this moment as a fresh start. With all of the changes he'd been through since the spring of 1993, he really felt like a different person and player and figured he should wear a different number.

Still, after a rocky start, it wasn't long before Michael proved to everyone—including himself—that he hadn't lost an ounce of his magic on the court. In his fourth game back, against Atlanta, Michael went for a trademark game-winning clutch shot—and sank it. His confidence building, Michael went on to dominate the Bulls' next game against their old rivals the New York Knicks, who'd beaten the Jordan-less Bulls in the previous season's play-offs. Michael poured in the baskets, ending up with 55 points—the record for that season. In the final seconds of the game, with the score tied at 111, Michael had the ball, and spectators guessed he'd take the last shot. As he moved toward the basket with his usual speed and grace, that guess seemed correct. But the Knicks defenders closed in on him, and Michael remembered what had made the Bulls so strong—their ability to trust one another in situations like this. So with just several seconds remaining on the clock, Michael tossed an expert pass to center Bill Wennington, whose resounding dunk gave the Bulls the win.

---

66*Playing [basketball] with [Michael]—it's like saying you played baseball with Babe Ruth.*99

—STEVE KERR

---

Michael was back, all right—back, and totally on fire!

Of the 17 regular season games the Bulls played after Michael's comeback, they won 13 and advanced to the play-offs. "It felt really good to be back out there on the basketball court, with a different outlook about life and how I approach each and every day," Michael reflected on his return. "I was making *myself* happy [this time]."

Within four days of Michael's number 45 Bulls jersey going on sale at the United Center, nearly 2,000 were sold.

Michael was hungry for another championship, but he knew it would be tough. He and his teammates were still adjusting to his own return and to the departure of forward Horace Grant, who now played for the Orlando Magic, plus the addition of Toni Kukoc, from Croatia. Still, the Bulls managed to eliminate the Charlotte Hornets in the first round of the play-offs, moving on to meet the Magic. Along with facing former teammate Grant, Michael and his Bulls were also up against the Magic's talented guard Penny Hardaway and giant center Shaquille O'Neal, a rising NBA superstar. After losing the first game of the series Michael came onto the court for the next game wearing his old number. "Twenty-three is just me," he said.

Unfortunately, the familiar jersey wasn't enough to power Michael and his teammates to another championship. Orlando defeated Chicago in six games, ending the Bulls' season. The disappointment stung, but Michael was confident that the following year would be different. "I'd like to think we were a rebound away, a power forward away, a Horace Grant away," he commented after the loss. Michael knew by now that he could trust his coach and the team's management to take care of that. What about any holes in his own performance? "I made a promise to myself that come next year, I'd be ready for this game."

He'd be ready, all right—no matter what it took! Michael spent hours on grueling workouts that summer, getting in his best shape ever even while filming his first feature film. *Space Jam* was a combination of live action and animation in which Michael—playing himself—costarred with Bugs Bunny. In the movie Bugs Bunny and other cartoon characters kidnap Michael and bring him down to their Looney Tunes world to get his help defeating their cartoon nemeses on the basketball court. Michael showed his playful side in the film, even taking a few stabs at his own low moments in baseball and his competitive spirit.

*I decided that I loved the game too much to stay away.*

—MICHAEL JORDAN, ON HIS COMEBACK

But off the movie set Michael was all business. He only agreed to take part in the filming under the condition that the producers provide a fully equipped gym nearby for him to work out in during his breaks. Michael invited fellow NBA players to

In 1996 *Sport* magazine named Michael the top athlete of the second half of the century.

the gym to scrimmage with him throughout the summer, making sure he wouldn't be the slightest bit rusty at the start of the next season. "I knew why these guys showed up," he said later. "They wanted to learn and to try to get a feel for the way I played. I knew their strategy. But they didn't know I was doing the same."

Meanwhile, just as Michael had expected, the Bulls management made a few changes to help the team to another championship. Before the start of the 1995–96 season the Bulls signed power forward Dennis Rodman, who had once been part of the Pistons team that had dogged Michael's Bulls at the play-offs year after year. Rodman had a reputation for being a rebel—he dyed his hair different bright, wild shades every night, wore gold jewelry on the court, and constantly challenged authority. In many ways he was the opposite of the always well-behaved, conservatively dressed Michael. But the two players shared a love of the game and a passion to win, and that was all Michael needed from a teammate. Well, that—and of course talent and skill! Luckily Rodman was one of the top rebounders in the game, exactly what Michael had said was missing from the Bulls.

"I couldn't wait for the 1995–96 season to start," Michael recalls. "I knew my game had come back with all the work I put in over the summer. I felt like a kid coming out of college with something to prove. The consensus was that I had lost a step. But there was no stopping us." The season opener was the first evidence of that, with Michael contributing 42 points and Dennis making 11 rebounds to give the Bulls their 105–91 win over the Charlotte Hornets. Michael was still putting himself through tough workouts to regain the conditioning he'd lost during his time away from basketball and was just as hard on himself mentally. When someone asked him if he felt he was still the best player in the league, Michael responded, "I'm not even the best player on this team."

While Michael wouldn't rest until he *could* say that about himself, it was a rush to be surrounded by such strong players, with Scottie Pippen taking off on the court and Dennis Rodman now leading the league in rebounding. The three-pronged attack of Michael, Scottie, and Dennis was downright lethal to opposing teams, and the Bulls continued to rack up the victories. As the All-Star break approached, the Bulls had an astounding 42 wins and only five losses. The 1971–72 Lakers team held the record for the best NBA season ever with 69 wins, and the whispers started up as everyone wondered—did this year's Bulls team have what it took to get the magical 70?

In Michael's mind there was no doubt. And on April 16 the Bulls arrived at the Milwaukee Bucks' home arena, the Bradley Center, ready to clinch the record. Eighty-six points later the Bulls had their seventieth win of the season, over the 80-point effort of the Bucks. The Bulls finished their regular season with a 103–93 defeat of the Washington Bullets on April 21, giving them a staggering record of 72 wins and 10 losses in the 1995–96 season.

"That was the best rhythm any Bulls team I played for had for an entire season," Michael later said. The evidence went beyond their impressive number of team wins—Michael recaptured the MVP award, while Phil Jackson was named Coach of the Year. Meanwhile Michael was joined by both Scottie and Dennis on the All-Defensive first team, a rare occurrence in the NBA for three players on the same squad. Still, as happy as Michael was with both his own play and the stellar performance of his teammates during the regular season, his sights were now set on one thing—another championship. "I want to grab back some of the respect I lost last year," he admitted. "I've played a full year and I have a chance to redeem myself. We have a chance to redeem ourselves."

The Bulls shook off exhaustion from their demanding season to take on the Miami Heat in the first round of play-offs, knocking them out in three straight games. Next came old rivals

> **❝**I've seen every basket that Michael's made as a professional. You think you see him do something he's done before, and then you say no, this is something he made up that's different.**❞**
>
> —CHICAGO TELEVISION ANALYST JOHNNY "RED" KERR

the New York Knicks, but the Bulls stayed tough, defeating them in five games. The pressure heated up as the Bulls faced their opponents in the Eastern Conference finals, the Orlando Magic, who had handed them a painful defeat in the previous year's play-offs. "I don't think the job is going to be easy," Michael remarked. "They're a year older, but we have more understanding about each other's talents and have a better continuity about each other. Hopefully, that's enough."

The question was soon put to rest. Michael's Bulls proved they were back and better than ever, completing a four-game sweep of the Magic that included some stunning accomplishments. Dennis Rodman grabbed an amazing 21 rebounds in the first game, while the team's strong defense held the Magic to only 67 points in game three, the second-lowest score in play-off history. Scottie Pippen poured in 27 points in that game, leaving Michael without any concern over his own "mere" 17 points. Still, Michael couldn't help stepping up his offense in the next and final game of the series, giving spectators what they were there for with a 45-point game. More satisfying to Michael than all the individual contributions and moments of the series was the larger fact that the Bulls had really become an unstoppable force of teamwork.

With the Eastern Conference title under their belt, the Bulls now moved on to the NBA finals, where they would take on the Seattle Supersonics. Seattle had enjoyed a solid season of 64 wins, but the Bulls were heavily favored to win the championship. For Michael this goal had a great deal of added personal meaning. "[Winning] would be very, very gratifying," he said at the time, "a tribute to my father and the motivation he had provided. Even though he hasn't been around, that's part of my motivation every day, to go out and make him proud of what I've done."

Following through on his words, Michael made every effort to make his father proud, and his teammates didn't let him down.

Michael was only the second player in NBA history to be named All-Star Game MVP, regular season MVP, and Finals MVP all in one year! He accomplished the impressive "triple" for the first time during the 1995–96 season.

The Sonics put up a good fight, halting the Bulls' three-victory run by taking games four and five. But in the crucial game six, the Bulls used everything they had to shut down Seattle, and the final score of 87–75 gave the Bulls the win—and the championship!

After the buzzer sounded, Michael grabbed the basketball and collapsed onto the court facedown, clutching the ball to his chest. His teammates quickly surrounded him, trying to pull him up to celebrate. But Michael wasn't ready to face them just yet; he was too overcome with emotion over the immense significance of this moment, a championship that meant so much more than the previous ones.

It was Father's Day.

"I know he's watching," Michael told a reporter after regaining his composure. In the locker room the tears came freely, and Michael announced with pride that this trophy was for his father. "I think it was a signal to some degree that he was there with me," Michael later said of the timing of the championship victory.

Having proved to himself, his teammates, and the rest of the world that he was still the best, there was only one thing left for Michael to do—keep right on playing the game he loved.

# Chapter Eight

# Another "Three-peat"... and Another Good-bye?

The Bulls picked up right where they'd left off when the 1996–97 season began, winning their first 12 games. The team again went into the All-Star break with only a handful of losses, and Michael and Scottie were honored after the All-Star game in a special ceremony where they were named among the NBA's 50 Greatest Players.

To Michael's disappointment, the Bulls fell short of matching their previous season's record of 72 wins. Still, this year's 69 victories tied the Lakers for second best in the regular season, and Michael was again the leading scorer in the league, moving up to fifth place on the NBA's all-time scoring list. Dennis Rodman had also repeated as the number-one rebounder in the NBA, and the Bulls entered the postseason ready to prove they hadn't lost their champion edge.

A 1997 *Wall Street Journal* poll rated Michael as the third-best-liked man in America, behind Colin Powell and Tiger Woods.

As expected, the Bulls defeated each of their play-off opponents, advancing to the NBA finals for the second straight year. This time they would face the Utah Jazz, led by stars John Stockton and Karl Malone, nicknamed "the Mailman" because he could be counted on to deliver big. Before the start of the finals Malone was named regular season MVP. It was all too familiar for Michael—being pitted in the finals against a team whose star had beaten him for the award. Malone had acknowledged Michael when he accepted the honor, saying, "I thank Michael for letting me borrow [the MVP] for one year."

Still, Michael's competitive streak was as fierce as ever. One sportswriter predicted that "Michael will just have to settle for the championship trophy." And Air Jordan wanted to prove him right.

The series opened on Sunday, June 1, at the United Center in Chicago. The two teams battled it out for most of the game, neither pulling far ahead of the other. With only seconds remaining on the clock, the game was tied at 82 points when Karl Malone was fouled. Michael watched his opponent take the foul shots with his heart in his throat, knowing that the free throws could cost the Bulls the game. But amazingly Malone missed both attempts!

As soon as the second shot bounced off the rim, Michael was in action, diving for the ball and then calling an immediate time-out. This was crunch time, and he knew it. The Bulls had less than 10 seconds to get off a basket, or else the game would go into overtime. And crunch time was *Michael's* time. "I love the end of the game," he once said, "because it comes down to that one moment where it's all in my hands."

When the game started back up, the Bulls made sure to do exactly that and get the ball into Michael's hands. Michael whipped his body around as he freed himself of Jazz defenders, then launched a jump shot just under the final buzzer. It was good—and the Bulls won, 84–82!

Chicago fans chanted, *"MVP, MVP,"* to honor the player they felt deserved the award, and a disappointed Karl Malone admitted, "He made his [shot] and I missed mine. It's hard to argue with that."

The Bulls went on to take the second game of the series 97–85, a victory Michael credited to his team's strong defense. "Defense wins championships," he pointed out. "If you look at our team, we're a defense organism. . . . How we got here hasn't been on our offensive capabilities. It's been our defense."

However, the Jazz countered with their own tough defense in the next two games, holding Michael to 22 points in game four and tying the series at two games apiece. The Bulls were in danger of losing their championship title, and Michael knew that the fifth game would be critical.

What he didn't know was that it would be the most difficult game he'd ever played in his life.

---

*66I'm still in the same mode of trying to win championships, and at the same time I'm trying to have fun, too. Everything is fun. I played for fun for nine straight years. We happened to win championships.99*

—MICHAEL JORDAN

---

Michael woke up in the early hours of the morning on June 11 with what felt like the beginnings of the flu and felt so horrible that he couldn't get back to sleep. As the day progressed and game time approached, Michael's symptoms only grew worse. He arrived at Utah's Delta Center weakened from a high fever but determined to play. "I had never seen [Michael] as sick," Scottie Pippen recalls. "I didn't even think he could get his uniform on."

In fact, despite Michael's best efforts to convince his coach, teammates, and even himself that he could make it through the game, he later realized just what a huge risk he'd taken that day with his health and even his life. "I could have died for a basketball game," he related. "I played that game on heart and determination and nothing else. I didn't have any food, any energy, any sleep, or anything else." Michael was severely dehydrated but still drinking coffee (which causes further dehydration) to keep himself awake enough to function on the court. "There were times in the third and fourth quarters that I felt like I was going to pass out. I remember thinking, 'Get this game over so I can lie down.'"

The Jazz took advantage of Michael's weakness, charging forward to a large lead in the second quarter that inspired the TV announcer to predict that the game would be a "blowout." But Michael drew deep within himself, playing off his pure will to succeed, and somehow managed a staggering 38 points despite his illness. His final basket was a three pointer in the last minute of play that pulled the Bulls ahead and allowed them to finish with a win of 90–88.

Michael collapsed into Scottie Pippen's arms as the buzzer went off and was hurried to the locker room, where he was given fluids to hydrate his body. Meanwhile stunned spectators were left to gawk at the unbelievable display they'd just seen. "The effort he came out and gave us was incredible," Pippen agreed. "He showed how much of a professional he is. . . . He really gave us the performance we needed, and there's nothing else to say except, 'He's the greatest.' He's the MVP in my eyes."

---

*66[Michael has] showed us he's the best basketball player in the world.99*

—NBA COMMISSIONER DAVID STERN, WHILE PRESENTING MICHAEL WITH THE 1997 FINALS MVP TROPHY

---

After the energizing boost of game five, the Bulls returned home to the United Center for the sixth game of the series, feeling confident and ready for another championship. Michael's health was drastically improved, and he and his teammates played well—but so did the Jazz. With less than a minute left the score was tied at 86. The Bulls had the ball and called a time-out to plan their final play. That would mean getting the ball to Michael, right? After all, the game was on the line. But Michael knew the Jazz defense would suffocate him. He instead trusted teammate Steve Kerr with the shot, and Kerr kept his nerves under control just long enough to hit the two pointer. Who could dare let a teammate like Michael Jordan down?

The Jazz had one last chance to push the game into overtime, but Pippen intercepted their inbound pass and fed the ball to Toni Kukoc for a buzzer shot that gave the Bulls a four-point victory and their second straight championship—their fifth NBA title in seven years!

It wasn't much of a surprise when Michael was named MVP of the finals, but he was quick to share the glory with his teammates, especially Scottie Pippen. "He deserves [the award] as much as I do," Michael insisted. Scottie had played a great season and a great finals series, but it was obvious to everyone after what Michael did in game five that he was on an entirely different level, giving everything he could for his team, even when it seemed like he had nothing left.

---

**❝**I was around when Michael Jordan, the greatest player ever to play the game, played. It's something I'll always appreciate.**❞**

—Kevin Johnson, Phoenix Suns

---

"I didn't want to give up, no matter how sick or how low on energy I was," Michael later explained about his performance in that game. "I thought positive and did whatever I could do. I felt the obligation to give that extra effort so we could be [back in Chicago] for the fifth championship."

Michael had left so much of himself on the court that some people wondered if he would return to the Bulls the following year. But when the 1997–98 season began, Michael was there,

The Gatorade "Be Like Mike" commercial, released in August 1991 after Michael won his first championship, was so popular that it was brought back in February of 1998 for the All-Star game. This time Michael had a celebrity supporting cast singing along to the lyrics "I wanna be like Mike," including women's soccer star Mia Hamm, sportscaster Ahmad Rashad, and two of Michael's good friends—Larry Bird and Bugs Bunny. "All of us, in some way, want to be like Mike," explained Gatorade's vice president of marketing Sue Wellington.

ready for another winning season. Unfortunately, the Bulls were missing another key player as Scottie Pippen sat out the first 35 games while healing from surgery on his right foot. The team's rhythm was shaken, and their record was uneven. Critics began to hint that Michael, whose thirty-fifth birthday was in February 1998, was showing his age. But Michael disagreed. "I feel I'm playing my best basketball. . . . Earlier, I had more reckless abandon and was more athletic. Now I think I show more savvy out there."

With Pippen back in the lineup the Bulls picked up some speed, finishing the season with a 62–20 record. Michael won his tenth scoring title and became the oldest player to be named regular season MVP, as well as only the third player in history to receive the honor five times. Even more meaningful to Michael, the award was presented by basketball great Bill Russell. "I've always respected my elders, learned from them and tried to maintain the excellence of the game that they provided," Michael said solemnly. "For [Bill] to come here today is truly a trophy in itself."

But there was already another trophy on Michael's mind— a 1998 championship win would give him and the Bulls their *second* three-peat of the decade!

The Bulls swept the New Jersey Nets in the first round of the play-offs, then shut down the Charlotte Hornets in five games. The Indiana Pacers put up more of a struggle in the Eastern Conference finals, stretching the series to seven games, but the Bulls did what they needed to do in game seven and moved on to the NBA finals.

The Utah Jazz was back for round two, hoping to rewrite history and come away with this year's championship. They

Always searching for a new record to break, Michael became the first player to achieve a triple double (breaking into double digits in the three categories of scoring, rebounds, and assists) in an All-Star game at the 1998 game, with 14 points, 11 rebounds, and 11 assists.

fought the Bulls every step of the way, and the series again went to six games. But in the final seconds of game six Michael came through with two baskets in a row to give the Bulls a tight one-point lead that would clinch the game 87–86, giving the Bulls the win and the championship. The second shot was the one that left spectators gaping—first Michael stole the ball from Karl Malone, then he faked out defender Byron Russell and launched a beautiful jumper that sailed through the air with a perfect arc, ending in a triumphant *swish*.

The moment the buzzer sounded, the Bulls went crazy. Michael was engulfed in an embrace by Phil Jackson, who cried out in pure joy, "Oh my God, that was beautiful—what a finish!"

Jackson's words were echoed by many that day, followed by an increasingly persistent question—had that basket been the finish of not only the game and the 1998 championship, but of Michael's professional career in basketball?

---

❝*His game is beautiful to watch—not just effective in an athletic sense, but theatrically* beautiful.❞
—Sports commentator Bob Costas

---

86

# Chapter Nine

# His Airness Forever

**M**ichael's final shot in the championship game against Utah had barely sunk through the hoop when television viewers across the country heard the solemn words of the game's commentator—*"That may have been the last shot Michael Jordan will ever take in the NBA."*

Could it be true? Was Air Jordan really grounded for good this time?

Michael kept quiet during the owners' lockout that delayed the start of the 1998–99 basketball season, supporting his fellow players in their demands for better contracts. Once a compromise was reached between the owners and players and the season was finally about to begin, Michael shared the news that by then came as little surprise—he was retiring, again.

"It was difficult," Michael admitted, "because you're giving up something that you truly, truly love. My love for the game is very strong. It's hard to give up that love." But Michael was emotionally drained and mentally exhausted, and he felt he needed to take a step back and focus on life with his wife and children. "Being a parent is very challenging," he said candidly. "If you have kids, you know that. I welcome that challenge and I look forward to it."

Michael held a question-and-answer session after delivering his speech, and as expected, he was asked if this retirement, unlike the last, was 100 percent final.

"I never say never," Michael replied. "But it's 95, 99.9 percent." Why not 100 percent? reporters pressed. "Because it's my one percent and not yours," Michael threw back.

Michael's absence from the world of basketball was mourned all over again. Magic Johnson lamented, "It's a loss for basketball, but for kids, too, in terms of not being able to see a superb role model in action."

The tributes poured in, including one from Hall of Famer Jerry West, once a star guard on the court and now vice president of the Los Angeles Lakers. "He could have been one of the greatest players ever [even] if he never dunked a basketball," West said. "Michael might have been a better defensive player than an offensive weapon." Michael was especially psyched to hear West's praise because being respected as a complete player, not just someone who could score, was always a big deal to him. Also, he looked at West as someone who shared a similar approach to the game. "If there is one player I would have liked to play against in his prime, it would have been Jerry West," Michael wrote in his book, *For the Love of the Game.* "From what I have read about Jerry and from what others have told me, he played the game a lot like I did."

But it was time for Michael to adjust to life off the court, as West and other retired players had all had to do. Michael easily filled his time enjoying the company of his wife, Juanita, and their three children, who mean the world to him. He spent long hours on the golf course, devoting his full attention to the hobby he'd first gotten hooked on as an NBA rookie. Michael also had the opportunity to become more heavily involved in the charities he'd supported over the years, including the James R. Jordan Boys and Girls Club and Family Center, particularly close to his heart. Meanwhile Michael was still in constant demand to make commercials for the numerous products either endorsed by him, like Gatorade, or actually using his name, like the Michael Jordan cologne and Nike clothing line.

But despite his busy schedule, something was missing. By January 2000 Michael could no longer bear being on the sidelines of the basketball world, and he accepted a position as president of Basketball Operations for the Washington Wizards (formerly the Washington Bullets—the team Michael had played

> **❝**No matter how long I play, it'll never change—
> basketball's a part of me. I play because I love the
> game. I'm living my fantasy.**❞**
>
> —MICHAEL JORDAN

in his first regular season NBA game with the Bulls back in 1984). The job allowed him to be involved in the game from a new angle, and he enjoyed the work a lot. But how long could Michael be this close to the sport he loved more than anything without suiting up himself?

Obviously not long!

Over the 2001 summer whispers and rumors started that Michael was thinking about an incredible second comeback, at age 38. Feeding the suspicion was the fact that Michael had hired his former Bulls coach Doug Collins to coach for the Wizards. Did he hire Collins because he would be comfortable *playing* for Collins? Apparently so.

In September, Michael made it official, releasing a brief statement that he was signing a two-year contract with the Wizards. "I am returning as a player to the game I love," he said. "I'm not coming back for money, I'm not coming back for the glory. I think I left the game with that, but the challenge is what I truly love."

Washington Wizards owner Abe Pollin immediately shared his excitement over Michael's announcement. "The greatest player in the history of the game is joining my team, and for that I am extremely honored and pleased," Pollin told the media. But many sports fans were outraged. How could Michael do this to his legacy? He had left the game on such a beautiful note, with that game-winning basket against Utah in the 1998 finals. Why mess with that?

---

**66**In my life I don't know if I ever saw another athlete with such a remarkable set of qualities of mind, body, and spirit.**99**

—President Bill Clinton

---

Michael found such logic amusing and also slightly frustrating. He was a person, not a legacy, and what was the point in not living his life in order to preserve some frozen image on a television screen? Michael loved basketball—it was in his blood—and he missed it. As long as it was possible for him to play, he wanted to be out there playing.

Then came the next question—*was* it possible? Even Michael admitted that he wouldn't be able to perform the way he had in his prime, but he was confident he had something to contribute. Now he just had to prove that to everyone else—a challenge Michael had enjoyed his entire life.

The Wizards' first game of the 2001–02 season was an away game at Madison Square Garden in New York, against Michael's onetime rival the Knicks. While the Knicks handed the Wizards a disappointing two-point loss, with a final score of 93–91, Michael still led his team in scoring with 19 points. Critics focused on the shots he missed and the moves he would have made in the past, but other commentators noted how close the Wizards—a team that had been struggling in recent years, finishing the 2000–01 season with a record of 19 wins and 63 losses—had come to beating the higher-ranked Knicks. Clearly Michael's presence was giving the Wizards a much needed boost, and hopes were strong that the season would only get better from there.

Michael did not disappoint. His joy at being back on the court was boundless, and even with the limitations of his age he

---

66*The basketball court for me, during a game, is the most peaceful place I can imagine. . . . Being on the court is truly very much like meditation for me. . . . During the game, for one of the few times in my life, I feel like I'm untouchable.*99

—MICHAEL JORDAN

---

In 2000 ESPN named Michael the athlete of the century.

could still outscore and guard many of his opponents. Michael insisted that he was not "chasing stats" and instead just playing out of love for the game. But Michael, being Michael, still broke records. He could probably break them in his sleep! On December 29 in a game against the Charlotte Hornets, Michael scored a whopping 51 points, the most points ever scored by one player in a game at the MCI Center. He was also the oldest player in NBA history to score 50 or more points in a game. Michael's thirty-ninth birthday gift came in the form of one more record—his 22.9 points-per-game average during the season was the highest ever for a player age 39 or older. And while he no longer led the league in scoring, he did come second to just one player—superstar center Shaquille O'Neal—in the number of field goals produced in 48 minutes, beating out younger talents Chris Webber and Allen Iverson. Meanwhile Michael was up to some of his old tricks, hitting game-winning clutch shots at three different Wizards games, all against teams he had viewed as hot rivals while playing for the Bulls—the New York Knicks, the Phoenix Suns, and the Cleveland Cavaliers.

However, Michael—as always—prized team accomplishments above his own individual achievements. And his work with the Wizards, as both a strong player on the court and a team leader off, helped the squad to a highly impressive 18-game turnaround for the 2001–02 season. Michael was satisfied that the team had worked out a rhythm together that wasn't just about his presence. "I wasn't trying to overshadow them," he said at the end of the season. "I was trying to complement them—because they're our future."

On January 4, 2002, Michael scored his 30,000th career point in a game against—of all teams—the Chicago Bulls! Michael became the fourth player in NBA history to rack up such a huge number of points, and he did it in 960 games, coming in a close second to Wilt Chamberlain's record of 941 games.

While Michael spent a large part of the season frustrated by a knee injury that forced him to miss a total of 22 games, he still showed the meaning of dedication to his rookie teammates, playing through the pain when he could. After sitting out some games in late February and early March while recovering from surgery, Michael rejoined the Wizards on the court in late March, coming in off the bench instead of starting so that he could conserve his energy. On March 29, 2002—the 20-year anniversary of his famous game-winning shot in the UNC championship win—Michael scored a game-high 34 points in just 26 minutes of playing time. His performance helped the Wizards to a victory over their talented opponents, the Milwaukee Bucks, and showed that even two decades after the game that had made him famous, he was still a basketball powerhouse. "Michael has been that anchor for us, every single night," Coach Doug Collins shared with the media, affirming Michael's importance to the team.

With Michael Jordan on the team, the Wizards went from being twenty-second in the league in game attendance in 2000–01 to the top spot in 2001–02. Seventy-nine of the Wizards' 82 games of the season were sold out, including all 41 home games.

Having silenced the doubters, Michael could focus on his health and preparing for the 2002–03 season. Michael's second year with the Wizards had a new twist—shortly before the season began, the team's management hired Patrick Ewing (who had just retired as a player) to join the staff as an assistant coach. Patrick saw the chance to boss around his longtime rival as an added bonus to the job, joking that he'd ride Michael as hard as Michael had always ridden him. Patrick even teased fans with the comment that if Coach Collins needed him, he'd be happy to sign a short-term contract for a couple of days and come onto the court in his position as center. Michael couldn't have been happier about the chance to play for—and maybe even *with*—Patrick.

# Epilogue

# Like Mike

On July 3, 2002, moviegoers across the country flocked to theaters to see a new movie opening that day—*Like Mike*. The film features actor-rapper Lil' Bow Wow as Calvin Cambridge, a young boy living in an orphanage whose love for basketball is unfortunately much stronger than his skills at the game. Then one day a pair of high-top basketball sneakers is donated to the orphanage. The sneakers, Calvin is told, used to belong to "some basketball player." When Calvin discovers the initials M. J. inside the shoes, he realizes to his amazement that he's now wearing the sneakers once worn by the greatest basketball player ever—Michael Jordan!

After an incident one night involving a bad lightning storm, the shoes become charged with a magical power that allows Calvin to play like his hero Michael Jordan whenever he wears them. Calvin is suddenly able to master all kinds of amazing moves on the court—including dunking on players who tower over him. Sound familiar?

Michael doesn't appear in the movie, though various NBA players followed his lead in *Space Jam* and gave acting a try in *Like Mike*. However, the mystique of Michael Jordan's legendary greatness is at the heart of the film, proving that even though by 2002 Michael was reaching the end of his professional basketball career, he was still by far the most respected player in the league. *Like Mike* came in third at the box office its opening weekend—the important July 4 holiday weekend—grossing $20.1 million in five days, a solid performance for a movie of its kind, especially against the major summer blockbusters. The movie's popularity was no surprise to anyone familiar with the success that seems to come with any project tied to Michael.

Michael's commercials have brought in tons of money for the various products he endorses, from Ball Park franks to Hanes men's underwear. His restaurants in Chapel Hill, North Carolina, Washington, D.C., and Mohegan Sun, Connecticut (all named after him), are doing great business. Five best-selling videos about Michael were compiled into one DVD in 2001, called *Ultimate Jordan*, which jumped off the shelves. Even more impressive—Michael was the star of his own IMAX movie, *Michael Jordan to the Max*!

But still, as much as Michael enjoys the movies, restaurants, and commercials, the one place where he most wants to make a difference has been and always will be on the basketball court. And just as Michael's sneakers lead Calvin to basketball glory in *Like Mike*, Michael remains an inspiration to every basketball player in the world, from the five-year-olds dunking in *their* trash cans to accomplished players in the pros.

Michael will play the game he loves for as long as he can, always giving everything he has on the court. But he's eager to see what the next generation of basketball players will do. "The evolution of greatness doesn't stop with me just as it didn't stop with [Elgin] Baylor, Dr. J, Larry Bird, or Magic," he says. "The nature of evolution is to continue. . . . Somewhere there is a little kid working to enhance what we've done. It may take a while, but someone will come along who approaches the game the way I did. He won't skip steps. He won't be afraid. He will learn from my example, just as I learned from others."

This is the most important legacy Michael feels he can leave with those who love the sport of basketball as deeply as he does—something that has kept him going for his entire life and brought him to the incredible heights he has reached:

A challenge.

# CAREER STATS

| Season | Team | Games | Rebounds | Assists | Steals | Blocks | Points | Season average |
|--------|------|-------|----------|---------|--------|--------|--------|---------|
| 1984–85 | Chi. | 82 | 534 | 481 | 196 | 69 | 2,313 | 28.2 |
| 1985–86 | Chi. | 18 | 64 | 53 | 37 | 21 | 408 | 22.7 |
| 1986–87 | Chi. | 82 | 430 | 377 | 236 | 125 | 3,041 | 37.1 |
| 1987–88 | Chi. | 82 | 449 | 485 | 259 | 131 | 2,868 | 35.0 |
| 1988–89 | Chi. | 81 | 652 | 650 | 234 | 65 | 2,633 | 32.5 |
| 1989–90 | Chi. | 82 | 565 | 519 | 227 | 54 | 2,753 | 33.6 |
| 1990–91 | Chi. | 82 | 492 | 453 | 223 | 83 | 2,580 | 31.5 |
| 1991–92 | Chi. | 80 | 511 | 489 | 182 | 75 | 2,404 | 30.1 |
| 1992–93 | Chi. | 78 | 522 | 428 | 221 | 61 | 2,541 | 32.6 |
| 1994–95 | Chi. | 17 | 117 | 90 | 30 | 13 | 457 | 26.9 |
| 1995–96 | Chi. | 82 | 543 | 352 | 180 | 42 | 2,491 | 30.4 |
| 1996–97 | Chi. | 82 | 482 | 352 | 140 | 44 | 2,431 | 29.6 |
| 1997–98 | Chi. | 82 | 475 | 283 | 141 | 45 | 2,357 | 28.7 |
| 2001–02 | Was. | 60 | 339 | 310 | 85 | 26 | 1,375 | 22.9 |
| TOTAL | | 990 | 6,175 | 5,322 | 2,391 | 854 | 30,652 | 30.1 |

# AWARDS

ACC Rookie of the Year, 1982

*The Sporting News* College Player of the Year, 1983, 1984

Naismith Award, 1984

Wooden Award, 1984

Olympic gold medal winner, 1984, 1992

NBA Rookie of the Year, 1985

Slam-Dunk Champion, 1987, 1988

Scoring Champion, 1987, 1988, 1989, 1990, 1991, 1992, 1993, 1996, 1997, 1998

Steals Champion 1988, 1990, 1993,

Defensive Player of the Year, 1988

NBA regular season MVP 1988, 1991, 1992, 1996, 1998

All-Star Game MVP 1988, 1996, 1998

NBA Finals MVP 1991, 1992, 1993, 1996, 1997, 1998

# BIBLIOGRAPHY

Greene, Bob. *Rebound: The Odyssey of Michael Jordan.* New York: Viking Penguin, 1995.

Gutman, Bill. *Michael Jordan: A Biography.* New York: Pocket Books, 1999.

Halberstam, David. *Playing for Keeps: Michael Jordan and the World He Made.* New York: Broadway Books, 2000.

Jordan, Michael. *For the Love of the Game: My Story.* New York: Crown Publishers, 1998.

Lovitt, Chip. *Michael Jordan.* New York: Scholastic, 1998.

Lowe, Janet. *Michael Jordan Speaks: Lessons from the World's Greatest Champion.* New York: John Wiley & Sons, 1999.

Raber, Thomas R. *Michael Jordan: Returning Champion.* Minneapolis: Lerner Publications Company, 2002.

# WEB SITES

ESPN.com

http://msn.espn.go.com/main.html

*The on-line partner to the cable sports channel has archives of articles and interviews featuring Michael throughout his career in basketball.*

Michael Jordan: Official Web site

http://jordan.sportsline.com/

*Michael's official site is chock-full of information on his life, professional career, charity involvements, and corporate sponsorships.*

Wizards: The official site of the Washington Wizards

http://www.nba.com/wizards/

*The official site of the Washington Wizards team features bios, stats, and up-to-date information on Michael's latest NBA accomplishments.*

# FILMOGRAPHY

*Michael Jordan: Come Fly with Me.* NBA Entertainment, 1989.

*Michael Jordan's Playground.* NBA Entertainment, 1990.

*Michael Jordan: Air Time.* NBA Entertainment, 1992.

*Michael Jordan: Above & Beyond.* NBA Entertainment, 1996.

*Space Jam.* Warner Bros., 1996.

*Michael Jordan: His Airness.* NBA Entertainment, 1999.

*Ultimate Jordan.* USA Films, 2001

# INDEX